21st Century Skills Library

COOL SCIENCE CAREERS

FIRE INVESTIGATOR

Ann Heinrichs

Cherry Lake Publishing
Ann Arbor, Michigan

CHERRY
LAKE
Publishing

Published in the United States of America by Cherry Lake Publishing
Ann Arbor, Michigan
www.cherrylakepublishing.com

Content Adviser: Daniel J. Ellis, MS, IAAI-CFI, Evergreen Park Fire Department

Photo Credits: Cover and pages 1, 8, and 13, ©SHOUT/Alamy; pages 4 and 21, ©Peter Casolino/Alamy; page 6, ©Dale A. Stork, used under license from Shutterstock, Inc.; page 14, ©Tom Grill, used under license from Shutterstock, Inc.; page 17, ©Sylvia Cordaiy Photo Library Ltd/Alamy; page 19, ©Monkey Business Images, used under license from Shutterstock, Inc.; page 24, ©RubberBall/Alamy; page 27, ©Blend Images/Alamy

Library of Congress Cataloging-in-Publication Data
Heinrichs, Ann.
Fire investigator / by Ann Heinrichs.
    p. cm.—(Cool science careers)
Includes index.
ISBN-13: 978-1-60279-310-1
ISBN-10: 1-60279-310-7
1. Arson investigation—Juvenile literature. I. Title. II. Series.
TH9180.H45 2009
363.25'9642—dc22   2008029293

*Cherry Lake Publishing would like to acknowledge the work of
The Partnership for 21st Century Skills.
Please visit www.21stcenturyskills.org for more information.*

TABLE of CONTENTS

CHAPTER ONE

CLUES AMONG THE ASHES

Working at a fire scene can be dangerous. Fire investigators often wear hard hats to protect their heads while searching for clues.

Chris gazes across the smoldering rubble. Two families once made their home on this site. Now all that remains is a jumble of blackened memories—a bookcase here, a doll there. Firefighters had rushed to the late-night blaze, sirens screaming. They spent hours dousing the flames. Was it an accident? Or did someone set the fire on purpose? Sorting through the debris, Chris spots a charred gasoline can. It wasn't just a fire. It was arson!

Chris is a fire investigator, a detective who investigates how fires start. Arson is deliberately setting a fire that destroys a building or other property. It's a serious crime, and it can be deadly serious. If someone dies in the blaze, the offense is not just arson. It becomes murder.

Fire investigators such as Chris start to work as soon as a fire has been put out. Using their investigative skills, they find the origin and cause of the fire. They know how flames travel from one place to another. That leads to the fire's area of origin. Then, studying the fire-damaged remains, they figure out what started the blaze.

The investigator's first task is to check for accidental causes. Many things can start a fire by accident. It could be lightning, careless smoking, or careless use of candles. Maybe a stove exploded or a heater was too close to the

Many fires start in kitchens. Investigators use their skills to determine whether or not a fire started accidentally.

curtains. The building may have had a gas leak or faulty electrical wiring. Or maybe a child was playing with matches. If the fire was an accident, it's not arson.

After ruling out accidents, the fire investigator goes on to look for other clues. Those clues may become valuable evidence of a crime. Searching for clues is not often as easy as finding a gasoline can. Investigators may run across some object the arsonist dropped or left behind, such as glasses or a cigarette lighter. The smoke detector or fire alarm might have been turned off. There might be traces of an accelerant—a fuel, usually a liquid, that burns fast and makes fire spread quickly. Suppose people died in the fire. Why couldn't they get out? This can lead to chilling discoveries. The investigator may find blocked escape routes or a locked bedroom door.

Next, fire investigators work with the police and other law enforcement agencies to find a suspect. They question people to find out who might have a motive. Why do arsonists set fires? Many do it to get even with someone. Some want to kill the residents or to cover up a murder scene. Some commit arson as a hate crime against people of a religious or ethnic group. And many arsonists are just wild kids who set fires for a thrill.

In an arson investigation, anything can become evidence—even ashes.

One common motive for arson is insurance fraud. Most property owners buy insurance on their homes or businesses. If the building is damaged or destroyed, the insurance company pays the owner to make up for the loss. A property owner who needs money might burn his own building to collect on the insurance.

Investigating a fire can take months. The investigator gathers information at the scene, runs tests, interviews witnesses, and follows leads. Finally, when all the information is in, the investigator writes up a report. After someone is charged with arson and arrested, the investigator testifies at the trial as an expert witness.

How do fire investigators know what they know? Traditionally, they have relied on experience. They gained practical knowledge as they sifted through the ashes. When they trained others, they passed on their knowledge by word of mouth. With years of experience, each investigator developed his or her own insights into the telltale signs of arson. Many of those insights proved true over time. But others have been challenged by scientific research.

Fire research took a big leap forward in the 1980s. Scientist John DeHaan began conducting tests on fire behavior. He built full-scale test fires and analyzed what

happened. Scientists also began to understand flashovers. A flashover occurs when heat and gases from a fire build up in an enclosed area. Suddenly the whole area **ignites**. Flashovers create some of the same burn patterns once believed to be signs of arson. These developments provided valuable scientific facts for fire investigators. Still, some investigators stood by their traditional ways of detecting arson.

Then some judges began overturning arson convictions.

Armed with new scientific information, lawyers were able to raise serious questions about investigators' conclusions. Fire investigators were accused of using "junk science" instead of real science. This led to a greater push for scientific investigation. In 1992, the National Fire Protection Association (NFPA) issued *NFPA 921: Guide for Fire and Explosion Investigation*. Updated every 3 or 4 years, it became the basic handbook for fire investigations.

At the same time, computer modeling was becoming an important investigation tool. Scientists developed computer software that could model, or duplicate, fire behavior. Computer fire models can reconstruct actual fires and show how they grow and spread. They calculate temperature, smoke development, flame spreading, time to flashover, and other conditions.

Once again, the court system put more pressure on fire investigators. In the 1993 U.S. Supreme Court case

Daubert v. Merrell Dow Pharmaceuticals, the court ruled that expert witnesses' testimony must be based on reliable methods.

The *Daubert* ruling unleashed a flurry of debate among fire investigators. That debate is still going on today. Investigators with decades of hands-on experience feel their opinions are valid. Others believe scientific evidence is the only way to keep innocent people from going to jail. Many investigators say that the best fire investigation combines both science and practical knowledge. That may be true. But scientific evidence will surely carry more weight in the courtroom as time goes on.

CHAPTER TWO

HUNTING DOWN THE EVIDENCE

*Investigators wear masks to block out dust and other
particles that could be harmful to inhale.*

Fire investigation can be long, hard, dirty work.
Investigators spend hours rooting around in the rubble
that used to be someone's home or business. They risk
their lives, too. Some investigators have fallen to their
death through unstable floors and stairways. In spite of the

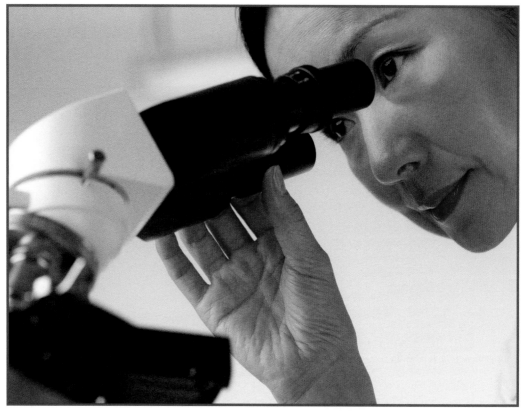

Lab technicians and other experts analyze evidence from fires.
They are an important part of an arson investigation team.

dangers, fire investigators are dedicated to their job. They want to hunt down evidence and help capture arsonists.

Weather and time don't stop an investigation. Fire investigators work night or day. They work in all kinds of weather, from freezing cold to sweltering heat. They may arrive on the scene when a fire is still blazing. Even after the flames have died down, heat, smoke, and sparks may still be hazards. So investigators might need to use protective gear such as respirators, safety goggles, and fireproof coats, pants, gloves, and boots. As they climb through mountains of rubble, they may have to lift heavy objects out of the way.

Collecting evidence is a big part of the job. Fire investigators dig through debris and carefully remove burned remains of carpeting, flooring, furniture, and other materials. Then they number each item, package the materials, and send them to a forensic lab. There, forensic scientists test them for traces of accelerants and other chemicals. They may also test for fingerprints. Any containers for gasoline, alcohol, or lighter fluid are also sent to the lab. So are any objects the arsonist may have left behind. It can be hard to sort out real evidence from worthless scraps.

Investigators also take photos or videos of fire scenes. Sometimes they study blueprints of a burned building to see where rooms, doors, closets, and stairs used to be. They might even reconstruct the fire scene to figure out what happened. To do this, they build a full-sized model of a room, set it on fire, and study how the fire develops.

Interviews are another big part of the job. The investigator questions the property owner, family, friends, and neighbors. Do they know of anyone who might have a motive for setting the blaze? Did anyone see suspicious people or activities in the area? The property owners themselves must be checked

Trained arson dogs can smell traces of accelerants, even if they have been diluted by water used to put out the flames.

out, too. Do they have a motive for harming or killing the residents? Are they in financial trouble? Is their business failing? Investigators get information from insurance companies and banks to help answer these questions.

After gathering information, the investigator writes up a report. It includes basic details such as the date, time, and location of the fire. Also included is an evidence list, along with the results of lab tests. There is information about building damage, injuries or deaths, witnesses, and suspects. Photos and videos are attached.

The fire investigator's report goes to the police, the fire chief, and the property owner. If enough evidence points to a suspect, the police make an arrest. Then the investigator works with attorneys, going over details of the report. Finally, the investigator testifies at the arson trial.

Many different investigators may take part in an arson case. City fire departments and police departments have fire investigators. In many states, the state fire marshal has its own investigators. Sometimes they are joined by investigators from the U.S. Bureau of Alcohol, Tobacco, Firearms and Explosives (ATF). Insurance companies hire fire investigators, too. All these people work together to solve the case. Sometimes they help bring an arsonist to justice. In other cases, they help set an innocent person free.

CHAPTER THREE

LEARNING THE TERRITORY

What are some skills that firefighters could carry over into a career as a fire investigator?

Would you like to be a fire investigator? Get ready for a long haul. There is no quick and easy way to walk into this career!

Most fire investigators start out working as firefighters or law enforcement officers. Almost no one becomes a fire investigator without experience in one of these fields. You might begin your career path by working as a volunteer firefighter. Then you'll start to understand how fires behave.

If you're interested in this career, you would enroll in your state or local fire training academy to become a firefighter.

After working as a firefighter for a while, you may find that fire investigation appeals to you. In most states, the state fire marshal or state fire commission offers programs that train firefighters to be investigators. The requirements for enrolling vary by state. Usually a firefighter must have at least 5 years' experience on the job. College courses in fire science or criminal justice are often required, too.

Future law enforcement officers get their training through the local police academy. Like firefighters, they may work in law enforcement for a few years before deciding to specialize in fire investigation. Then they may take the same state training program offered to firefighters.

Some fire investigators start their careers as fire protection engineers. Though it isn't necessary, many fire protection engineers have experience in fighting

At a fire academy, students learn about fires and ways to put them out.

fires. They learn about fire behavior in their college

studies. The University of Maryland, Oklahoma State

University, the University of California at Berkeley, and

Worcester Polytechnic Institute in Massachusetts all have

highly respected fire protection engineering programs.

Because courts are becoming more demanding, it can

be wise to enroll in a nationally recognized **certification**

Every year, more than 70,000 fires rage across millions of acres of forestland. According to the National Interagency Fire Center, lightning causes about 16 percent of these fires, which account for almost 70 percent of the wildland burned each year. The rest are caused by carelessness and arson.

In some ways, investigating forest fires is similar to investigating building fires. Investigators interview witnesses to find out about motives or suspicious people and activities. But evidence in forest fires presents special challenges. For example, burn patterns appear on trees and stones instead of floors and walls. The National Wildfire Coordinating Group (NWCG) decided that standards were needed specifically for investigating forest fires. In 2001, it developed a training program that leads to certification as a Wildland Fire Investigator (WFI).

program. Two private organizations certify people as fire investigators. One is the International Association of Arson Investigators (IAAI). It offers a Certified Fire Investigator (CFI) program. The National Association of Fire Investigators (NAFI) offers a Certified Fire and Explosion Investigator program. It uses *NFPA 921* as a training manual.

After completing one of these programs, some people stay with their local fire or police departments. Others go to work for companies that investigate fires, arsons, and explosions. Insurance companies hire investigators from companies like these.

Certain national government agencies also provide training in fire investigation. For example, the U.S. Fire Administration's National Fire Academy in Emmitsburg, Maryland, has fire investigation courses. The Federal Bureau of Investigation (FBI) offers arson training at its academy in Quantico, Virginia. And the ATF conducts a CFI program for its own employees, as well as state and local fire investigators.

Certification programs cover a wide range of subjects. Students learn about such things as fire chemistry and behavior, fire stages from beginning to flashover, fire scene analysis, burn patterns, and computerized fire modeling. Information about hazardous materials, explosives, car fires, and electrical fires may be covered, too. There are courses on collecting and handling evidence, photographing fire scenes, interviewing witnesses, writing reports, and testifying at trials.

All of this knowledge leads toward one goal—removing dangerous arsonists from the community.

CHAPTER FOUR

THE FUTURE: FEELING THE HEAT

Good communication skills are important when fire investigators testify in court. They must be able to clearly explain their findings.

Fire investigators are feeling the heat. Often their expert testimony is the key to convicting an arsonist. But courts continue to raise the standards for expert witnesses. Investigators are expected to back up their testimony with scientific principles. Their conclusions must be based on experiments that can be repeated with the same results. Otherwise, a court might not accept their testimony. Clearly, investigators of the future will need more training in science-based skills.

Training methods are already becoming more high-tech. One new training tool is the interFIRE-VR system. (*VR* stands for **virtual reality**). Arson investigators can use interFIRE-VR on a laptop computer in their local offices. Through virtual reality, they analyze a fire scene, collect evidence, interview witnesses, draw conclusions, and present the case at a trial. The system prompts the user to draw on all possible sources of information in the investigation. CFITrainer.net is a Web site that offers online training in a variety of subjects related to fire investigation.

Fire research is heading in many new directions. Researchers are now working on a system in which investigators can take digital photos of the fire scene and

load them into a laptop computer. Then they mark out the fire damage and burn patterns. The marked images are sent by satellite to a computer site where the information is analyzed. The computer sends back many possible versions of what could have caused the fire. The investigator would examine each version and decide which fits the scene best.

Computer fire modeling is becoming more complex all the time. One new development is the Fire Dynamics Simulator (FDS). Like many other models, it reconstructs a fire scene and displays it on a computer screen. But FDS goes much farther. It divides a room or building into thousands of separate cells, along with

*Computers are very helpful tools for fire investigators. They can
help experts determine the cause and behavior of a fire.*

walls, floors, furniture, and other objects there. For each

cell, FDS shows the temperature, burn rate, and other fire

conditions in that exact location. This shows investigators

how the fire grew and spread.

Forensic labs are also improving their methods of testing

for accelerants. Sometimes two different labs come up

with different results. One finds the presence of accelerants on a material, while the other one doesn't. Scientists are developing new testing methods that are more efficient than ever. They separate the chemicals in a material and identify those that are accelerants. In the future, these methods will become standard practices for all forensic labs.

Field testing is another wave of the future. Investigators will be able to take portable forensic labs right to the fire scene. Then they can test materials for accelerants immediately.

The ATF opened its Fire Research Laboratory in Beltsville, Maryland, in 2002. It conducts scientific research on reconstructing fire scenes and analyzing evidence. The lab hopes to establish scientific standards that any court will accept. This would be a giant step forward. It would give fire investigators the hard-core tools they need in the courtroom. Then it will be the arsonists who are feeling the heat.

SOME FAMOUS FIRE INVESTIGATORS

Vytenis (Vyto) Babrauskas (1946–) was the first person to earn a doctoral degree in fire protection engineering. He is a physicist and fire scientist who invented the cone calorimeter. It's now the primary instrument for determining how fast objects such as furniture burn. Babrauskas has also done important research on the deadly gases released in fires.

John DeHaan (1948–) has conducted extensive research on the behavior and effects of fires. He wrote the updated book *Kirk's Fire Investigation*, the most widely used textbook on the subject.

Gerald Hurst (1937–) is a chemist and fire consultant who investigates fire origins and causes in arson cases. An opponent of nonscientific investigation, he often testifies in arson trials.

Paul Kirk (1902–1970) published *Fire Investigation* in 1969. As the first science-based text on fire investigation, it ushered in the scientific investigation of fires.

John Lentini (1952–) is a nationally known fire researcher and arson expert who wrote *Scientific Protocols for Fire Investigation*. As an expert witness, Lentini has helped many people falsely accused of arson to prove their innocence.

James G. Quintiere(1940–) is a fire researcher and safety engineer. He worked in the Fire Science and Engineering Division of NIST and is currently on the faculty of the Department of Fire Protection Engineering at the University of Maryland. He has investigated many fire disasters and is the author of many books and journal articles on fire investigation.

GLOSSARY

accelerant (ak-SELL-ur-unt) a fuel, usually a liquid, that burns rapidly and makes fires spread quickly; common accelerants include gasoline, alcohol, and paint thinner

blueprints (BLOO-prints) drawings of a building's layout, with white lines on a blue background

certification (sur-tuh-fih-KAY-shun) an official declaration that someone has passed certain tests or achieved a certain standard

debris (duh-BREE) fragments of something that has been destroyed or broken

evidence (EV-uh-duhnss) things that suggest or prove a fact

expert witness (EK-spurt WIT-niss) someone with special knowledge or skills who testifies at a trial

forensic lab (fuh-REN-zik LAB) a place with the equipment and conditions for doing scientific studies on crime-related materials (*lab* is short for *laboratory*)

fraud (FRAWD) obtaining money by deceiving someone

ignites (ig-NITES) catches fire

motive (MOH-tiv) a person's reason for doing something

research (REE-surch) detailed scientific study and testing

suspect (SUS-pekt) someone believed to be guilty of wrongdoing

virtual reality (VUR-choo-uhl ree-AL-uh-tee) a computer technique using a three-dimensional scene with which people can interact

FOR MORE INFORMATION

Books

Ford, Jean. *Explosives and Arson Investigation*.
Philadelphia: Mason Crest Publishers, 2006.

Harmon, Daniel E. *Careers in Explosives and Arson
Investigation*. New York: Rosen Central, 2008.

Latham, Donna. *Fire Dogs*. New York: Bearport Publishing, 2005.

Stewart, Gail B. *Arson*. Detroit: Lucent Books, 2006.

Websites

ArsonDog.org
www.arsondog.org/shared/news_art1.asp
For more information about arson dogs

Fire Safety
www.dos.state.ny.us/kidsroom/firesafe/firesafe.html
Learn more about fire safety and arson dogs

SmokeyBear.com—Get Your Smokey On
www.smokeybear.com
Click on the Smokey Kids link for games, stories, and other
fun ways to learn about wildfire prevention

USFA Kids
www.usfa.dhs.gov/kids/flash.shtm
Visit this U.S. Fire Administration site to learn more about fire safety

INDEX

ABOUT THE AUTHOR

Ann Heinrichs is the author of more than 200 books for children and young adults. They cover U.S. and world history and culture, science and nature, and English grammar. Ann has also enjoyed careers as a children's book editor and an advertising copywriter. An avid traveler, she has toured Europe, Africa, the Middle East, and East Asia. Born in Fort Smith, Arkansas, she now lives in Chicago. She enjoys biking, kayaking, and flying kites.